The Let's Talk Library™

Let's Talk About Feeling Worried

Melanie Ann Apel

The Rosen Publishing Group's
PowerKids Press™
New York

To Melissa McGurren, my Moonmate, and morning radio smile...with thanks for everything, the other Mel

Published in 2001 by The Rosen Publishing Group, Inc.
29 East 21st Street, New York, NY 10010

First Edition

Book Design: Maria Melendez

Photo Credits: pp. 4, 7, 8, 11, 12, 15, 16, 19, 20 by Myles Pinkney.
A warm special thanks to Waring Magnet Academy of Science & Technology.

Apel, Melanie Ann.
   Let's talk about feeling worried / by Melanie Apel.
     p. cm.— (Let's talk about library)
   Includes index.
   Summary: Defines worry and discusses ways in which it can be both beneficial and harmful.
   ISBN 0-8239-5622-9 (alk. paper)
    1. Worry in children—Juvenile literature. [1. Worry.] I. Title: Let us talk about feeling worried.
  II. Title. III. Series.
   BF723.W67 A64 2000
   152.46—dc21

00-024769

Manufactured in the United States of America

Contents

Robin

Robin and her family are moving to a new town. Robin has to say good-bye to her friends. She is worried that she will not make friends in her new town. She is worried that she will not like her new school. In the new house, Robin will not have to share a room with her sister Amelia. Robin is excited about having her own room, but she is also worried that she will miss having Amelia nearby.

If you are moving to a new town, you will have to say good-bye to some friends. This is hard, especially if you are worried that you will not make new friends.

5

What Does It Feel Like To Worry?

When you worry, you feel **anxious**. Feeling worried makes you upset or **concerned**. Many different situations can make you feel worried. If you are moving to a new town, starting at a new school, or going to camp for the first time, you might worry about what will happen. Will you meet new friends? Will you like your new teacher? Will there be fun things to do at camp? It is okay to worry about how you will deal with a new situation. Everyone worries sometimes, even grown-ups.

6 *When you start at a new school, you might worry that you will not have anyone to sit with at lunch. It can take time to get to* ▶ *know people. Just be yourself and you will do fine.*

The Spelling Test

Erika is worried about the spelling test she has today. She feels like she needed more time to study. Erika does not think she will do very well on this test. This makes her feel like she has butterflies in her stomach. Her heart is beating fast. She feels a little sick. Erika wishes she did not have to go to school today. Then she would not have to take the spelling test.

◀ *Taking a test can make you feel worried. If you try hard and do your best, that is all anyone can ask of you.*

Scott's Bike

Scott wants to ride his bike, but he is worried. Last time he rode his bike, he fell off and scraped his leg. The other kids laughed at him. He does not want that to happen again. Scott is very worried about hurting himself. He is also worried about the kids in his neighborhood making fun of him. These things worry him so much that he has not taken a bike ride for two weeks.

It is hard to get back on your bicycle after falling off. If other kids laugh at you, they are the ones who are silly. ▶

It's Okay to Worry

It's not always a bad thing to worry. Maybe you fell off your bike because you were riding too fast. Now you are worried about going for another bike ride. You don't have to stop riding your bike. You can just be more **cautious** and ride slower. If you are worried because you have not studied for a test, you can make sure you are more prepared next time. That way you won't have to feel anxious when it comes time to take the test. Do not be hard on yourself if you make a mistake. Just use what you have learned to try and do a better job next time.

If you make a mistake, don't be afraid to try again. No one is perfect.

13

Dealing With Your Worries

Sometimes you can do things to make your worried feelings go away. You can visit your new school or camp before you start going there. Seeing a new place ahead of time can make you feel more comfortable. You can also ask for help with things that are worrying you. Ask your mother for help with your math homework if you are having trouble. Maybe your dad can take you to the pool a few extra times before you start swimming lessons. Your family loves you and wants to do all it can to make you feel better.

Ask your parent to help you do your homework. You will feel less worried, and you and your parent will ▶ have extra time together, too!

Talk About Your Worries

It helps to talk to someone about what is worrying you. Talk to your parents about your problem. A friend, teacher, or **guidance counselor** can help you feel better, too. Sometimes when you talk about something that is worrying you, it does not seem like such a big problem anymore. Just getting your feelings out in the open can make your worries seem smaller. No matter who you talk to, remember this person cares about you. He or she is ready to listen and might even have some great **advice** to offer.

◀ *If you are having a problem at school, talk to your teacher. He or she cares about you and wants to help you work things out.*

Waiting for Mom

Carol is waiting for her mother to pick her up at a friend's house. It is getting late. She looks out the window of her friend's house. Her mother's car is nowhere in sight. Carol wonders where her mother is. She is worried about her mother. She is also a little angry. Carol wonders if her mother has forgotten about her.

If someone is late picking you up, you might think that something has happened to him or her. ▶
This can make you feel worried.

Worrying About Someone Else

It is natural to worry about the people who matter to us. Worrying all the time will not stop bad things from happening, though. If you worry all the time, you will make both you and the people around you anxious. The best thing to do is to let the people you love know that you worry when they are late meeting you or coming home. Ask them to call if they are going to be late. Tell them you will do the same. If you do this, everyone will worry less. This also shows **respect** for the people who mean so much to you.

◀ *Tell the people you love that you worry about them. They might not realize that something they do concerns you so much.*

21

Everyone Worries

Everyone worries at one time or another. We worry about our family and friends. We worry about how we will handle something we had trouble with before. We worry about what it will be like when we meet new people or move to a new place. Worrying can be good when it makes us use **common sense** so we do not hurt ourselves or anyone else. Try not to worry too much, though. Enjoy your life and trust that you will be able to deal with anything that comes your way!

Glossary

advice (ad-VYS) An opinion about how to handle a
   problem.
anxious (AYNK-shus) When you feel uneasy or worried.
cautious (KAW-shus) Being very careful.
concerned (KON-sernd) Feeling worried about something.
common sense (KA-mun SENS) When someone uses good
   judgment.
guidance counselor (GY-dins KOWN-suh-ler) Someone who
   helps students solve personal problems or problems with
   other people.
respect (ree-SPEKT) To think highly of someone.

Index